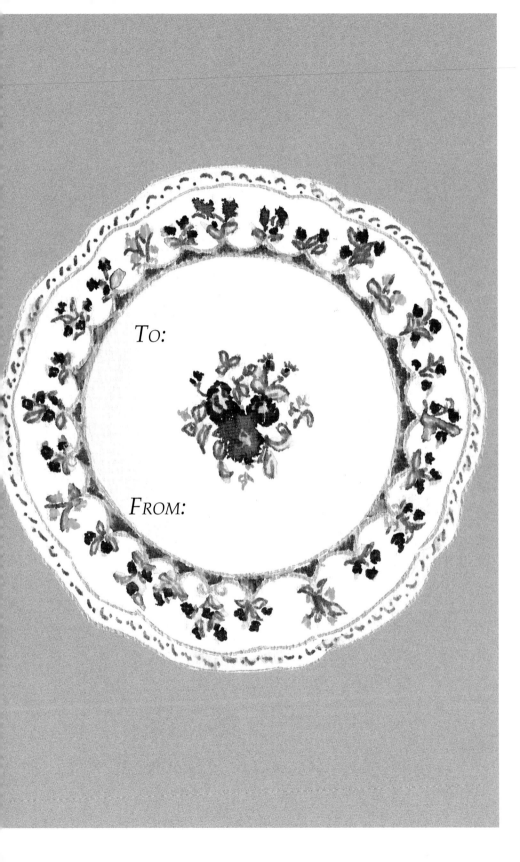

To:

From:

Smith & Daniel Marketing and Public Relations
Publishing Division
4981 Atlantic Blvd., Suite 9
Jacksonville, FL 32207
1-800-330-1325

ISBN 0-9630463-7-3

A GATHERING
OF FRIENDS

LORI ANDREWS IBACH

with illustrations by
S. PAIGE WILLIAMS

ACKNOWLEDGMENTS

A round of thanks to the members of my dinner group, whose recipes, parties, and companionship inspired me to write this book:

CINDY AND TODD JOHNSON
LAURIE AND DEAN SCOTT
KELLEY AND CHRIS WARD
KERRY AND STEVE WARREN

I am also indebted to my illustrator, **S. PAIGE WILLIAMS**, for her incredible talent which she so warmly and eagerly shared.

Finally, may I offer my respect and appreciation to my family and friends, whose assurance and love supported me throughout this adventure. In particular, I submit my deepest gratitude to my loving husband, **B. J.**, who served as my editor and constant motivator.

INTRODUCTION

I can remember the conversation vividly; my friend asked me what I thought about forming a dinner group with a few other couples in our area. My immediate reaction was "Wouldn't this type of entertaining happen naturally within our circle of friends? Why would we have to plan to have dinners together?"

Thankfully, her reaction was that a gathering of friends is not always easy in our busy world composed of accountants, lawyers, teachers, architects, entrepreneurs and interior decorators. We would be better off planning out time together months ahead to ensure that our schedules could reflect our social agendas as well as our work repertoires. Specifically, our calendars were to incorporate five dinner parties, one to take place in a different friend's home every other month.

My friend's idea began to make a lot of sense to me, and I was actually quite appreciative of the invitation to be a part of this quest for culinary companionship. Hence, with three more couples left to call, she directed her inquiries to the other wives regarding her desire to begin a dinner group. When all of the prospective chefs concurred with her idea, our group was formed.

Our gathering of friends is now in its second year with an incredible array of dining extravaganzas to our credit.

*This book is dedicated
to my parents,
Dennis and Susie Andrews,
and my brother, Marc,
for their
unconditional love
and support.*

CONTENTS

"A gathering of friends offers us security and
comfort in a world where companionship
and love of home must
once again become the focus of our interests."

- L. A. Ibach

Chapter One

FORMING A DINNER GROUP

I n February of 1994, I received a letter from "The Queen of the Microwave," our organizer's self-proclaimed nickname. The letter was the quintessential token of organizational tactics for our dinner group. She acknowledged that her "purpose of the letter was to map out the dates for the year and to set some ground rules for our dinner group."

Hence, her organizational schema was two-fold. First, she included a calendar denoting the dates of the prospective dinners. These dinner dates also alluded to the division of our culinary labor. The various courses were listed alongside of the names of the couples who were to prepare a particular course that evening. Thus, one knew ahead of time if he/she was to create a refreshing vegetable platter or to bake a decadent dessert.

Included is our actual schedule for the year, which has been amended with the generic headings of couple numbers 1-5 to make it easier for you to use this same organizational tool. Your dates and months may differ, but this chart will work for you!

SAMPLE SCHEDULE

February 27

Entree - Couple #1

Vegetable - Couple #2

Hors d'oeuvres - Couple #3

Dessert - Couple #4

Beverages - Couple #5

April 30

Entree - Couple #2

Vegetable - Couple #3

Hors d'oeuvres - Couple #4

Dessert - Couple #5

Beverages - Couple #1

June 25

Entree - Couple #3

Vegetable - Couple #4

Hors d'oeuvres - Couple #5

Dessert - Couple #1

Beverages - Couple #2

August 20

Entree - Couple #4

Vegetable - Couple #5

Hors d'oeuvres - Couple #1

Dessert - Couple #2

Beverages - Couple #3

October 29

Entree - Couple #5

Vegetable - Couple #1

Hors d'oeuvres - Couple #2

Dessert - Couple #3

Beverages - Couple #4

December 31

Dinner out on the town to give all chefs and hosts a reward for a fabulous year of dinner group!

In addition to the calendar, her letter also delineated "rules of the game." In other words, we needed to understand the objectives of our bi-monthly meetings. Her list of three rules established our bylaws for the proposed activities. The requirements were:

1. **The Entree Chef is the host.** As the host you have the creative control. You can choose a theme (see Chapter 3) if you want, but it is not necessary. Let everyone know ahead of time what you plan so compatible side dishes can be prepared.

2. **All dates are subject to change as necessary.** If you have a date conflict, contact the host and figure out an alternative date — then make sure everyone knows this new agenda.

3. **You must cook something you have never made before.** This requirement is, of course, on the honor system.

Having a list of rules that is succinctly written will avoid subjecting your newly acquired group members to any unnecessary anxiety attacks that could follow a list of greater length and restrictions. Of course, rules may vary, but objectives should be set to minimize any uncertainty concerning the rules!

For example, if rule number three had been omitted from our list, our culinary climate would differ greatly from the innovative climate that our dinner group offers. We thoroughly enjoy researching our recipe choices, as well as anticipating that those choices will be delectable on their first go-round.

Thus, have fun with your rules, but have rules!

SOME OTHER HELPFUL ORGANIZATIONAL HINTS:

•   Recognize that the hosts, the couple preparing the entree, have the hardest task. Therefore, make sure that their hosting date fits perfectly into their schedules. The other members' dishes aren't nearly as involved as providing the entree in addition to the dining facilities. Preparing for a dinner at your home is the most challenging assignment in a Dinner Group (see Chapter 2). However, I believe that it is truly the most rewarding task if you have an adequate amount of time to prepare for the gathering.

•   Make sure that all members realize that a meal is incomplete without a particular course. Thus, all couples must attend! The purpose of organizing dates months in advance is to ensure that these dates are sacred to the dinner group. Cancellations must be acknowledged far in advance to avoid infringing on the best interests of the entire group. Our group had a problem in this area, which was a difficult hurdle to overcome as we ended up losing a dynamic couple's participation in our gatherings.

•   Try to keep your dinner group at no more than 10 people. We have found that 10 people can still fit comfortably in our dining rooms. In addition, dividing the menu into five courses has worked very well. Our experience with five couples has been ideal!

"To share your home with others is to offer a warming cordial

composed of the finest ingredients."

- L. Λ. Ibach

Chapter Two

Hosting the Dinner Group

Although I have only hosted two dinners for our dinner group (we are in our second year), I have made a habit of hosting numerous other get-togethers prior to our dinner group's conception. I absolutely love the art of entertaining and welcome the opportunity to share with you the intricacies of party planning that dictate my normal preparation.

Step One: The Invitation

Primarily, once the date is set, it is your option to decide whether to send a written invitation for the dinner, or to simply make a phone call to the dinner group members. In the case of our dinner group, I have sent invitations for both parties held at my home. I feel that our dinner group is a special time together which warrants a proper invitation. A written invitation serves as a lovely precursor to the awaited evening. In addition, the formal invitation inhibits procrastination, as you must jump ahead to Steps Two and Three in order to provide the necessary thematic data for your invitation.

If a written invitation is not your style, a phone message will serve the same purpose for a less formal affair. Whatever the medium of invitation, the objective is the same — a reminder of your planned time together.

Step Two: That Special Recipe

After defining the proper time and attire in your invitation, you are free to explore the world of fine cuisine. My journey usually begins with the latest copy of *Bon Appetit* or *Gourmet*. If nothing makes my mouth water in either of those issues, I go through back issues of these magazines to reread my countless pages of dog-eared recipes. If I am still stumped, I'll hit the local bookstore for a new cookbook or magazine to add to my growing collection of cooking manuscripts.

Step Three: Thematic Unity

When my research is rewarded with a recipe that sparks my interest, I next consider the recipe's thematic qualities. Is it of a particular cuisine? Would it lend itself to a casual spring picnic, or is it better suited for a formal winter gathering? The thematic elements of a dinner define the ambiance of your gathering. Once established, it is important to relay this thematic knowledge to your fellow chefs so that their dishes will add to the overall impact of the occasion. If the host fails to provide adequate thematic information for the other group members, the menu could be a motley mixture of oddities rather than a symphony of complimentary dishes! Thus, it is best to provide your thematic data to your fellow chefs ahead of time, either in your written or verbal invitation.

STEP FOUR: A CREATIVE SETTING

Orchestrating a beautiful setting for your guests is half of the fun of having the dinner group in your home. A proper setting can transport you to the banks of the Seine for a Parisian ensemble or carry you to the verdant environs of your own backyard for a dinner amongst the glories of Nature. The setting allows your thematic choice to come alive. You are not only eating a particular cuisine, you are dining with the locals of your chosen region! The main components needed to enrich your setting correspond to the five senses:

- **Sight** — A visually stimulating environment with authentic props relating to your theme.
- **Smell** — The wafting aroma of a regional delicacy scenting the interior and/or exterior of your home.
- **Sound** — The musical notes set forth by your special sound system or entertaining musical guests.
- **Touch** — The textures and accoutrements of your table's decor that kinesthetically dictate the formality of the occasion.
- **Taste** — The succulent array of culinary treats that you and your guests have brilliantly assembled.

13

Step Five: To Visualize the Affair

Prior to making a trip to the grocery store, I map out the table setting and make a list of the other necessities that must be on hand for the dinner evening. This sketch and list pattern enables me to visualize the forthcoming evening to ensure that a key ingredient is not missing. I focus once again on the "Five Senses Theory" and check to make sure that everything is on my list. I have found that if I can visualize the setting and the meal ahead of time, I am not as panicky the day of the dinner. The creative legwork has been accomplished; I just have to put everything in its proper place for that evening.

Step Six: The Final Details

I usually prepare the table the night before the party. This frees up the day of the dinner for a last minute clean-up. Once the house is in order, I simply light the candles that are arranged throughout our home, begin the music, and attend to my entree as I anticipate the commencement of the evening.

SOME OTHER HELPFUL HINTS:

• Call your dinner group guests a couple of days before the party to make sure that you have the utensils that they need for their particular course. For example, if the beverage person is making cappuccino after dinner, do you have the necessary cups for everyone?

• If you plan to serve a particular course outside, make sure that the chef of that course is aware of this information. Some dishes are not conducive to outdoor entertaining.

• Try to get the majority of prep work for your entree accomplished prior to your guests' arrival. Your guests will also need to use your kitchen for final preparations of their dishes.

"A creative mind illustrates with the commanding spectrum of a rainbow, rather than a fabricated palette of ordinary hues."

- *L. A. Ibach*

Chapter Three

CREATING THE PERFECT SETTING FOR YOUR DINNER PARTY

To create a setting for your dinner is to summon your five senses to orchestrate an enchanting evening for all to enjoy. Represented here are accounts of some of the thematic settings that have enhanced our dinner group's special evenings. At the conclusion of this chapter is a recap of the thematic ideas presented in the commentaries of this chapter. My hope is that our ideas may offer you some creative   suggestions for your group's enjoyment.

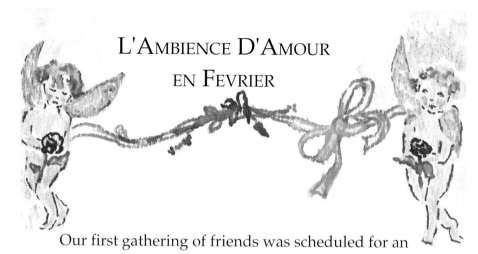

L'Ambience D'Amour
en Fevrier

Our first gathering of friends was scheduled for an evening in February, which lended itself nicely to a theme evoking the images of a romantic European vacation for two, or was that ten? Our dinner group's premiere journey was reminiscent of the most memorable part of any voyage — the delectable dining experiences shared with friends.

To set the stage for our European affair, the invitations were written in French to allude to the prescription of a french cuisine. The french culinary theme was interwoven with the intangible elements of amour (love), evidenced by the depiction of a cherub which adorned the right hand corner of the invitation. My objective for the setting of this dinner relied on an intermingling of these two themes. I decided that the food was to pertain to the European motif, but that my table setting should refer to the theme of amour.

With a chicken dish entree that emphasized the finest elements of French cuisine, a rich white wine sauce, home-grown herbs and fresh legumes, I relied on my friends' selections to round out the remainder of the European menu.

The real fun came in creating the romantic ambience for my guests. While perusing my bookshelves for an idea on how to incorporate the theme of love, I came across a book that spoke of the Victorian Period's focus on the art of having flowers denote a particular message. Since my table was sure to be set with a floral arrangement of some sort, I decided to select flowers according to their Victorian message. With a literary bouquet in hand, I placed a grouping of these flowers in chorus in an entry-way bouquet and singularly at each place setting.

Upon entry, each couple selected their favorite flower from the large arrangement in the entry-way and then found its match at the table. Once everyone found their seats marked by their chosen flowers, they sat according to the chair designated for the lady (Madame) or the man (Monsieur).

Once seated, each couple shared their flower's message that was written on the back of their place cards. For example, the couple who selected the iris informed us that the iris was known as the "messenger of love." The couple seated at the pink cabbage rose boasted that their flower was the "ambassador of love." The other flowers signified such qualities as truth, innocence, capricious beauty and simplicity.

Our first "gathering of friends" was a rousing success, enhanced by our floral harbingers of love!

DINNER IN A SPRING GARDEN

If I'm not entertaining or preparing for my teaching, I'm in the garden! Because of my passion for Mother Nature's offerings, I planned a dinner party this year around the setting of our backyard. This April gathering was to be a more casual affair than our winter European dinner. Its culinary theme was "Nature's Bounty," a tribute to the abundance of fresh vegetables that populate the produce markets in the spring.

With this in mind, I opted for a vegetarian course of Calzones, and I informed my fellow dinner group chefs that the cuisine was to be as light and fresh as a dew swept spring day.

Since April the 15th also preceded Peter Cottontail's yearly arrival, I incorporated an Easter egg hunt into the agenda for the evening. This dinner group party was to commence at 4:30 for the hunt and hors d'oeuvres and continue with cocktails until the calzones and side dishes were served at 6:OO.

Working around the possibilities of a holiday theme lends itself to a creative setting. Working with preexisting symbols and images conducive to a holiday setting is a simple way to spice up your entertaining backdrop. By merely placing a bunny or a colored egg at strategic places in your home, you can create the desired over-all effect of fluidity. It becomes much easier to carry your theme outside into your garden by merely adding these props to the table on the patio where the appetizers will be served.

With this accomplished, seek to make the inside mimic the outside; bring nature within! Why not place that rose topiary that usually adorns your patio in the middle of your dining room table?! Or nest that symbolic egg amongst a bed of alyssum that is tumbling out of tiny terra-cotta pots to accent each individual's place setting. Bringing the garden inside allows you to entertain in a garden setting in the evening, when you are ready to retire from an area that the mosquitoes have just found very attractive!

Our retreat into the natural world provided the perfect casual setting. I highly recommend a culinary afternoon in the garden. If Easter is in the forecast, don't pass up the chance to see adults scurry around your garden for the winning egg! That exhibition was a greater treat than the coveted chocolate bunny that our egg hunt winner received!

AN ITALIAN DINNER TO REMEMBER

The home of one of my dearest friends was the location of an Italian dinner beautifully orchestrated for 10. It is hard to forget the aroma that greeted us as we entered the home, whose walls resounded with the jubilant tones of Frank Sinatra. The smell was of a rich and tangy tomato sauce bubbling in the oven over the pasta shell trios that encased stuffed mixtures of cheese, spinach and meat sauce.

We noticed that our chef's home was void of the multitude of toys that occupy a home recently blessed with a baby. Her spotless home reassured those of us who are still without children that our dinner group evenings will continue to work with growing families.

Our host's table decor mirrored that of an Italian bistro. Nestled in her lovely home, we felt as though we were instead secluded amongst the waterways of Venice. The rich red tablecloth and crimson flowers were illuminated by candles that projected out of their bottled homes of Italy's finest Burgundies. The thematic element of color evident in all of these accoutrements set the stage for our evening of Italian reverie.

It was a pleasurable evening spent with friends and culinary delights that warmed our spirits with the same intensity as the battery of red elements that defined the decor!

A NIGHT OF FICTION

1995's dinner group festivities embarked on a new direction as our hosts donned fictional personas, Archibald Frath and Captain Mal respectively, and invited us on a suspenseful journey aboard *The Gilded Vessel*. *The Gilded Vessel* was the title of the Murder Mystery package our hosts purchased for our night of fiction.

As passengers on this vessel, we all arrived adorned in our appropriate flapper-era attire, anxiously awaiting the evening's forthcoming production. Perhaps the most distinguished entry was made by her Lady Nadya, entangled in a flowing scarlet boa, and her driver and companion, Miles, whose parcel of freshly baked french bread's aroma wafted through the vessel. Jules, the debonair Parisian jeweler, immediately presented himself to the latest guests, who were being escorted into the kitchen to deposit their bread and bundles of asparagus. Simultaneously, I (Bella) noticed the arrival of a superbly dressed duo: the sophisticated Lady Desiree and the affluent W. C. As pleasantries were exchanged, the final passengers arrived: the charming Lady Lucie and her mystery companion. With all passengers on board, the *Gilded Vessel* set sail for an evening of murderous mystery and delectable dining.

One way to recreate our fictional voyage is to purchase one of the numerous Murder Mystery games that are available. The game comes complete with descriptions for each person's fictional persona, a tape that introduces you to the objectives of the Murder Mystery and visual props such as maps and letters to read at the appropriate time during the evening. This package works very well with the dinner group format as each mystery round can be identified with a particular course in your dining repertoire.

If the hosts of the party provide you with a thematic setting to match the background information given, you are set for a theatrical evening! Our table looked like an enlarged representation of a CLUE game — candlesticks and possible murder weapons were strewn across the table.

The addition of culinary delights to this tablescape titillated our taste buds as we challenged our deductive reasoning skills with the game's investigative format. Our dinner group loved the creative composition of the evening. We all left our hosts' home reassured that this year's dinner parties would be as entertaining and as successful as our first year's adventures had been.

A Caribbean Escape

When our neighbors hosted a Caribbean dinner group party, a poem came to my occasionally literary mind. Robert Frost explored the dynamics involved in neighborly relations in his poem "Mending Wall." Frost's narrative account of his neighbor's statement "good fences make good neighbors," is meant to show the irony of his neighbor's outlook on friendly relations. It is my belief that if Frost could have lured his neighbor into a more agreeable relationship with some good home-cooking, perhaps his neighbor would have shunned the confinements of a physical barrier more readily! After all, it is amazing what an evening of culinary camaraderie can do!

Cooking a meal, or even a loaf of banana bread, for a neighbor shows that you care. Our neighbors have treated us on numerous occasions to their fantastic cooking. Their Caribbean influenced mahi-mahi entree was no exception. I guarantee that if Frost had made *Jerked Mahi-Mahi* for his neighbor, his neighbor's imposing wall would at least have had a gateway connecting the two homesteads.

With this in mind, let me add that this evening's gathering of friends was perhaps one of the finest culinary ensembles yet assembled by our panel of chefs. This is easy for me to say, as my duty that evening was beverages. Although I liked the quenching strawberry wine punch I made, it was the remainder of the menu that was so outstanding! The spicy fish entree was complemented beautifully by the subdued *Mushrooms Parmesan* which formed the perfect marriage with the *Fried Polenta.*

In addition to the culinary artistry exhibited at this gathering, our hosts also orchestrated a Caribbean backdrop that spoke directly to this maritime theme. Large palm fronds surrounded the dining table, which was decked out in scuba gear that surfaced on the vibrant Caribbean tablecloth. The tablecloth was a selection of fabric that enveloped the table beautifully in its flamboyant hues. A color-ful spectrum of terry towels (to serve as our napkins) enhanced the tablescape, providing a practical and textural supplement to the casual decor.

The setting's carefree style was mimicked in the musical notes of the Reggae music that our hosts provided.

Our neighbor's Caribbean dinner was a blissful tropical escape that enabled us to set aside our busy routines for an evening of camaraderie and fine cuisine. When your neighbor's home offers such a rejuvenating respite, you wonder why more neighbors aren't involved in the sharing of culinary gifts. Perhaps if they were, there would be fewer "walls to mend" and more hearts to tend.

A Recap — Ways to Increase the Thematic Impact of Your Setting

- An invitation serves as a thematic precursor to your evening.

- Unique floral arrangements that differ from the usual flowers in a vase ensemble.

- Symbolic holiday figures: bunnies, Santas, pumpkins etc. that when strategically placed and creatively assembled augment the thematic holiday presentation.

- Acquired knowledge of your thematic subject that is relayed to your guests in an innovative manner.

- The incorporation of an emotional element in your thematic composition.

- Individual place cards and unique menu cards that acknowledge each person's significance and course's contribution to your overall presentation.

- The inclusion of an activity that relates directly to the occasion's traditional sentiments, for example:

    An Easter Egg Hunt in the spring

    Caroling outing at Christmas

    Apple bobbing in the fall

    Croquet in the midst of summer

- The cuisine's representative locale that serve as the thematic focus for your decor.

- A monochromatic palette that unifies the setting and creates a particular mood. For example:

    Red — warmth and passion

    White — serenity and sophisticated simplicity

    Light Blue — tranquility and compassion

    Royal Blue — regal drama

    Yellow — uplifting and cheery

    Black — powerful and formal, especially when
    accented with white or gold

    Green — invigorating and fresh — a mirror of nature

- Sporting equipment as props that conjure up a popular pastime indigenous to your setting's locale.
- Textures in your tablescape that reflect the degree of formality of the occasion.
- A collection of items suggestive of your culinary region as a focal point for your table, mantel, hutch, etc.
- Nature's offerings that make a statement when brought indoors.
- Music that relates to a regional style, popular artist's heritage, or is reflective of the mood of the gathering.

"Cooking for others may very well be one of the most
delectable expressions of friendship."
- *L. A. Ibach*

Chapter Four

THE BEST RECIPES FROM OUR FIRST YEAR

With the organizational and thematic nature of a dinner group party understood, what remains are the fabulous recipes that reward your efforts! The recipes compiled in this book are divided into two formats: the "Best Recipes from Our First Year" and the complete "Menus from Our Second Year."

This chapter's recipes are the dishes that were chosen as our favorites from our first year of dinner group. Hence, these dishes are not meant to compose one complimentary menu, but rather to accentuate your chosen menu with one extraordinary dish! The selections in this chapter are surefire winners if your group decides that each recipe must be one that you've never made before. I am confident that these treasured recipes will also be amongst your group's favorites. So give these selections a try and happy cooking!

* Note: These recipes serve 10 people.

LAURIE'S SWISS CHEESE BREAD PUFFS
****

Ingredients:

1 C. milk

1/4 C. butter

1 C. flour (all-purpose or self-rising)

4 eggs

3/4 C. shredded Swiss cheese (3 oz.)

1/4 C. grated Parmesan cheese

DIRECTIONS:

Heat oven to 400 degrees. Heat milk and butter to a rolling boil in a 2 quart saucepan. Stir in flour. Stir vigorously over low heat until mixture forms a ball; about 1 minute, remove from heat. Beat in the eggs and continue beating until the batter is smooth and thickened. Beat in 1/2 C. of the Swiss cheese and the Parmesan cheese.

Drop spoonfuls onto greased cookie sheet. Bake on center oven rack until puffed and golden - approximately 30 minutes.

LORI'S SWISS CHEESE FONDUE

****

Ingredients:

1 garlic clove - halved

2 C. dry white wine

4 C. shredded Swiss Cheese

1/2 tsp. baking soda

2 TBSP. flour

1/4 tsp. cayenne pepper

1 tsp. garlic salt

2 TBSP. Brandy

DIRECTIONS:

1. Rub fondue pot with garlic and then discard garlic.

2. Pour wine into pot and simmer for 4 minutes. Do not boil!

3. In a bowl toss cheese, flour and baking soda.

4. Add cheese mixture 1/4 C. at a time to fondue pot.

5. Add cayenne pepper, garlic salt and Brandy to pot.

6. Heat at least for 5 minutes for flavors to develop.

7. Serve with fresh vegetables and french bread.

KELLEY'S STUFFED SHELLS (CHEESE AND FLORENTINE)
****

1 LB. Ricotta Cheese

1 C. shredded Mozzarella

1/4 C. grated Parmesan

1 10 oz. package frozen spinach (cooked and drained)

1 tsp. Italian Seasoning

20 jumbo shells, cooked a la dente

16 oz. of your favorite Spaghetti Sauce

  (perhaps try the homemade Spaghetti Sauce in Chapter 5)

Parsley sprigs for garnish

DIRECTIONS:

Mix the first 5 ingredients. Stuff 3 TBSP. of mixture into each shell.

In a 12X8 baking dish, spread 1/2 of the sauce. Arrange shells

stuffed sides up in sauce. Spoon remaining sauce over shells.

Cover with foil. Bake at 350 degrees for 35 minutes.

Sprinkle with parsley and serve.

* NOTE: FOR CHEESE STUFFED SHELLS, JUST LEAVE OUT THE

SPINACH AND REPEAT ABOVE DIRECTIONS. YOU WILL

WANT TO MAKE 20 SHELLS OF EACH VARIETY IN ORDER TO

HAVE ENOUGH SHELLS FOR TEN PEOPLE.

KERRY'S GROUPER WITH SHRIMP BUTTER CREAM SAUCE

****

Ingredients:

Sauce:

5 1/2 TBSP. unsalted butter, in all

2 TBSP. all-purpose flour

1/4 C. finely chopped onions

2 cloves of chopped garlic, or to taste

1 1/2 C. fish stock

3/4 tsp. salt

1/2 tsp. ground red pepper

1/4 tsp. white pepper

1/2 C. heavy cream

1 dozen peeled small shrimp, about 2 oz.

Grouper for 10 people (pan fried in seasoned flour mix)

DIRECTIONS:

To make **Shrimp Butter Cream Sauce**:

In a 1 quart saucepan melt 4 TBSP. of butter over medium heat. Whisk in flour with a metal whisk until well blended. Remove from heat and set aside.

Place the remaining 1 1/2 tablespoons butter

and onions in a 2-quart saucepan. Saute over high heat until onions are wilted, about 2 minutes, stirring occasionally. Add the stock and bring to a boil. Whisk in the salt and red and white peppers, then the butter-flour mixture; cook over high heat 4 minutes, whisking frequently. Add the cream and continue cooking and stirring for one minute, whisking frequently. Add the shrimp and continue cooking and stirring just until the shrimp turn pink, about 30 seconds. Remove from heat. Makes about 2 cups. Serve sauce over pan fried grouper.

Seasoning mix for frying:

1 C. flour

1 tsp. white pepper

1 tsp. onion powder

1 tsp. ground red pepper

1/2 tsp. garlic powder

DIRECTIONS FOR FISH:

Mix the flour seasoning mix. Dredge fish in mix and fry in oil (oil to come half way up the side of the fish) for a couple of minutes on each side until cooked through. Transfer cooked fish to plates and top with Shrimp Butter Cream Sauce.

Note: If you want extra sauce for your fish - double the recipe!

CINDY'S SOUR CREAM POUND CAKE

****

Ingredients:

(all ingredients should be at room temperature)

2 sticks of butter

3 C. of sugar

6 eggs

1/2 pint sour cream

1 tsp. vanilla extract

1 tsp. almond extract

1/4 tsp. baking soda

3 C. flour

1/4 tsp. salt

DIRECTIONS:

Cream butter and sugar in mixer. Add eggs one at a time. Add sour cream and flavorings; beat well. Sift dry ingredients together and add to creamed mixture. Beat for 5 minutes. Pour into a greased and floured tube or bundt pan. Bake at 300-325 degrees for 1 hour and 30 minutes or until done. Cool in pan for 5 minutes and then turn over onto serving platter. Serve garnished with fresh strawberries and vanilla ice cream.

"Dining amongst a 'gathering of friends' seasons a
menu's composition."
- L. A. Ibach

Chapter Five

MENUS AND RECIPES FROM OUR SECOND YEAR

This chapter offers your dinner group a sampling of our menus that we've relished so far this year. Each recipe given here serves 10 people; therefore, these recipes may be easily adopted into your group's repertoire.

I have enjoyed the written assembly of these recipes as it has afforded me the opportunity to relive some of our most memorable meals. In fact, I am sure that I will recreate these menus for future dinners — that is, as long as these meals are not dinner group related. Remember: I must always find a new recipe when a "gathering of friends" occurs!

A Night
of Fiction

Stuffed Clams Florentine

Shrimp in Puff Pastry

Asparagus with Herbs

White Wine of Choice

*Classic Raspberry
Cheesecake*

Frangelico

Stuffed Clams Florentine

****

Ingredients:

3 1/2 qts. cherrystone clams

1/2 C. dry white wine

1 10 oz. package fresh spinach

12 TBSP. butter

3 TBSP. finely chopped shallots

2 cloves of garlic, finely minced

1/2 C. finely chopped heart of celery

3 TBSP. dry white wine

2 tbsp. finely chopped parsley

1 TBSP. finely chopped tarragon

1 TBSP. finely chopped chives

1 C. fresh bread crumbs

1 egg yolk

salt and freshly ground black pepper

1/2 C. freshly grated Parmesan cheese

10 lemon wedges

DIRECTIONS:

Preheat oven to 425 degrees. Rinse the clams well under cold running water to remove all traces of sand. Place them in a four-quart kettle or saucepan and add the 1/2 C. dry wine. Cover closely, bring to a boil, and cook until clams open, five minutes or longer. Let the clams cool.

While the clams cook, rinse the spinach with cold water, shake to remove excess moisture, and place in a saucepan. Do not add additional water. Cover and cook until the spinach is wilted, eight to ten minutes. Stir, cover again, and cook about two minutes longer. Drain in a colander and cool.

Melt one-quarter cup of the butter in a skillet and cook the shallots, garlic, and celery, stirring. Cook about five minutes. Add the three tablespoons wine and simmer until all the wine evaporates.

Squeeze the spinach carefully but tightly to remove all the excess moisture. Chop the spinach, then add to the skillet and stir.

Remove the clams from the shells and reserve fifty to sixty clam shells. Strain the clam juice through the cheesecloth and reserve one-half cup. The remainder may be used for another purpose.

Using a butcher knife, chop the clams until they are fine. This should yield about one and one-half cups chopped clams. Add the clams to the skillet and stir.

Add the remaining butter, the parsley, tarragon, chives, bread crumbs, and reserved clam juice to the skillet. Add the egg yolk and mix well with a wooden spoon, then season with salt and pepper to taste. Cook briefly in the skillet. Use the mixture to fill the reserved clam shells. Sprinkle with Parmesan cheese and place, on baking sheets, in the oven. Bake 10 minutes at 425 degrees, or until the clams are piping   hot and golden brown. Serve hot with lemon wedges.

Shrimp in Puff Pastry

****

Ingredients:

6 TBSP. butter

8 artichoke hearts (2 cans)

16 oz. sliced fresh mushrooms

2 TBSP. dried parsley flakes

2 TBSP. garlic salt

2 10x15" sheets of frozen or fresh puff pastry

20 oz. Swiss cheese, sliced

24 jumbo shrimp, cooked, shelled and deveined

4 TBSP. grated Parmesan cheese

2 eggs, beaten

1 tsp. minced fresh parsley

DIRECTIONS:

Melt butter in a large skillet over medium-high heat. Add artichoke hearts, mushrooms, parsley flakes, and garlic salt. Saute until mushrooms are tender. Allow mixture to cool. Drain well. Set aside.

Oil a large rimmed baking sheet. Place puff pastry on baking sheet. Overlap Swiss cheese slices lengthwise along right half of pastry leaving a 1-inch border at the long edge and 1/2 inch border at each end. Arrange artichoke hearts over cheese, spreading evenly. Spoon mushrooms over cheese and artichoke hearts. Arrange rows of shrimp on top of mushrooms. Sprinkle 2 TBSP. of Parmesan cheese on top. Brush borders with half of the beaten egg.

Fold left half of dough over filling, pressing edges firmly with fork to seal (may be prepared up to 8 hours ahead at this point if kept covered and refrigerated.)

Preheat oven to 475 degrees. Brush pastry with remaining egg. Sprinkle with parsley and remaining Parmesan cheese. Bake for 10 minutes. Reduce oven to 375 degrees and bake until golden, about 15 - 20 minutes.

Asparagus with Herbs

****

Ingredients:

4 lbs. fresh asparagus

1 stick of butter (1/2 cup)

3 TBSP. mixture of dried herbs (basil, parsley and oregano)

DIRECTIONS:

Trim and wash off asparagus. Simmer asparagus in boiling water until tender — approximately 2 minutes. Drain and plunge into icy cold water to stop the cooking process. When ready to serve, melt butter in skillet and add herbs. Saute herbs for a couple of minutes and then add the asparagus. Heat through for two to four minutes. Serve immediately.

Classic Raspberry Cheesecake

****

Ingredients:

1 1/2 C. graham cracker crumbs

2 TBSP. sugar

1/4 C. plus 2 TBSP. butter or margarine, melted

1 tsp. grated lemon rind

3 (8oz.) packages of cream cheese, softened

1 C. sugar

3 eggs

1/2 tsp. vanilla extract

1 (16oz.) carton sour cream

3 TBSP. sugar

1/2 tsp. vanilla extract

Raspberry glaze (1 pint raspberries sliced with sugar to taste)

DIRECTIONS:

Combine graham cracker crumbs, 2 TBSP. sugar, butter, and lemon rind in a medium bowl; stir well. Press mixture firmly on bottom and up sides of a 9" springform pan. Bake at 350 degrees for 5 minutes; set aside.

Beat cream cheese at high speed of an electric mixer until light and fluffy; gradually add 1 cup sugar, beating well. Add eggs, one at a time. Stir in 1/2 tsp. vanilla. Pour cream cheese mixture into prepared crust. Bake at 375 degrees for 30 to 35 minutes or until cheesecake is set.

Beat sour cream at medium speed of electric mixer for two minutes. Add 3 TBSP. sugar and 1/2 tsp. vanilla; beat 1 additional minute. Spread sour cream mixture evenly over cheesecake. Bake at 500 degrees for 3 to 5 minutes or until sour cream mixture is bubbly. Remove cheesecake from oven. Let cool to room temperature. Top with a raspberry glaze of fresh raspberries and sugar. Chill at least 8 hours. To serve, carefully remove sides of springform pan.

Nature's

Bounty

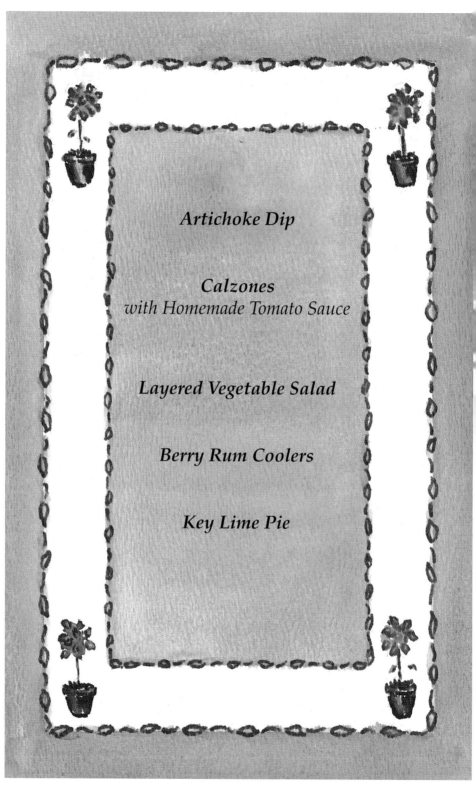

Artichoke Dip

Calzones
with Homemade Tomato Sauce

Layered Vegetable Salad

Berry Rum Coolers

Key Lime Pie

Artichoke Dip

****

1 (12 oz.) can artichoke hearts, chopped well

1 (4 oz.) jar marinated artichoke hearts, chopped well

1/2 C. cheddar cheese

1/2 C. sour cream

1/2 C. mayonnaise

1/2 C. Parmesan cheese

DIRECTIONS:

Combine all ingredients and cook at 350 degrees for 20 to 30 minutes or until hot and bubbly.

Serve hot with crackers, melba toast or corn chips.

Calzones
****

Ingredients:

1 oz. fresh yeast

2 1/2 C. lukewarm water

pinch of salt

pinch of sugar

6 C. all-purpose flour

1 TBSP. olive oil

Filling:

3 C. ricotta cheese

3 C. mozzarella cheese, grated

6 TBSP. freshly grated Parmesan cheese

6 eggs

salt and pepper to taste

DIRECTIONS:

Dissolve the yeast in the water and stir in the salt and sugar. Pour the mixture into the flour with the oil and mix to a dough. Knead until smooth and elastic - about 10 minutes. Cover with clear plastic wrap and leave to rise in a warm place until doubled in size.

To make the filing, mix the ingredients together, reserving 2 TBSP. of beaten eggs for glazing. Add plenty of seasoning. Knock back the risen dough and divide into 12 pieces. Roll a piece of dough out thinly on a lightly-floured surface to make an 8 inch circle. Place one-twelfth of the filling on the dough and wet the edges of the circle.

Fold one side of the circle over to make a semi-circle shape and seal the edges. Place on a baking sheet and brush with a egg yolk. Repeat with the remaining dough and filling. Bake at 450 degrees for 10-15 minutes. Serve warm with homemade tomato sauce (see recipe) on top of Calzone or to its side.

Homemade Tomato Sauce
****

Ingredients:

1/2 C. chopped onion
2 cloves garlic, minced
3 TBSP. olive oil
2 cans (1 lb. 4 oz. each) tomatoes, cut up
1 can (8 oz.) tomato sauce
2 cans (6 oz. each) tomato paste
1 C. water
2 tsp. basil
2 Tbsp. minced parsley
2 tsp. salt
1/4 tsp. pepper

DIRECTIONS:

Saute onion and garlic in olive oil. Add rest of ingredients and simmer over low heat for 1 hour minimum.

Layered Vegetable Salad

****

Ingredients:

4 C. torn romaine lettuce

1 C. fresh peas

1 C. shredded carrots

2 hard-cooked eggs, diced

6 slices bacon, crisply-cooked, drained and crumpled

3/4 C. shredded cheddar cheese

2 green onions sliced (white and green parts)

3/4 C. mayonnaise

1 1/2 tsp. lemon juice

1/2 tsp. dillweed

DIRECTIONS:

Place lettuce in the bottom of a clear glass bowl (8" diameter). Layer peas on top of lettuce, then carrots on top of peas. Arrange egg slices and bacon over vegetables. Top with 1/2 C. of the cheese and the green onions. Make dressing; combine mayonnaise, lemon juice and dillweed. Spread dressing over salad's entire surface. Sprinkle with remaining cheese. Cover and chill for 2-24 hours. Before serving, toss to coat the vegetables.

Berry Rum Coolers

****

Ingredients:

4 cans of frozen Tropicana Twisters

(Cranberry/Raspberry/ Strawberry)

Ice

Rum

DIRECTIONS:

Put frozen mix in blender and fill the empty Tropicana carton 2/3 full of rum. (A combination of rums works well, or one type of rum will suffice.) Add the rum to the blender along with ice to fill the blender. Blend and serve with a sliced strawberry on the rim of the cup. Each Tropicana carton makes approximately 4 drinks.

Key Lime Pie

****

Ingredients:

1 9" Graham Cracker Crust

1 14 oz. can condensed milk

3 egg yolks (do not use the whites)

1/2 C. key lime juice

DIRECTIONS:

Combine condensed milk, egg yolks and lime juice. Blend until smooth. Pour filling into pie crust and bake at 350 degrees for 10 minutes. Allow to stand for 10 minutes before refrigerating. Just before serving, top with fresh whipped cream and garnish with lime sections.

Caribbean Escape

Caribbean Sweet & Hot Dip

Jerked Mahi-Mahi

Fried Polenta

Mushrooms with Parmesan

Refreshing Strawberry Punch

Brandied Apple Pecan Tart

Caribbean Sweet and Hot Dip

****

Ingredients:
24 ounces of cream cheese, softened
1/2 C. orange marmalde
1/2 c. apricot jam
1/4 C. hot pepper sauce (Tabasco)
1/3 C. sour cream
3 TBSP. honey
1 TBSP. chopped fresh parsley
1 TBSP. lemon juice

DIRECTIONS:
In a bowl, combine all ingredients and mix thoroughly until smooth. Cover and refrigerate for a couple of hours (minimum) to "marry" the flavors. Serve with crackers.

Jerked Mahi-Mahi

****

Jerk Marinade Ingredients:
1 tsp. ground allspice
1/2 tsp. ground nutmeg
1/2 tsp. ground cinnamon
1/2 C. chopped scallions (green and white parts)
6 jalapenos, without seeds
1/2 C. distilled white vinegar
1/4 C. soy sauce
2 TBSP. vegetable oil
1 TBSP. salt
pinch of garlic powder
Mahi-Mahi for ten people

DIRECTIONS:

Combine all ingredients in a blender or food processor. Process or blend on the liquify setting for 2 minutes. Pour into a jar and refrigerate until ready for use. Jerk Marinade will remain good indefinitely as long as it is covered and kept refrigerated. To use the marinade, marinade chicken or fish for three hours or overnight (chicken only) at a ratio of 1 TBSP. per pound of meat. To make Jerk Sauce simply add 1/2 cup of distilled white vinegar to marinade recipe. Simmer for 15 minutes minimum and use as a condiment with grilled jerk treated meat.

Fried Polenta
****

Ingredients:
6 C. of milk
2 TBSP. unsalted butter
2 tsp. sugar
1 tsp. salt
2 C. stone- ground yellow corn meal
4 TBSP. unsalted butter
* For a more flavorful Polenta add sauteed onions, garlic and red peppers to the prepared Polenta mix. Add a dash of Tabasco, too!

DIRECTIONS:

Combine the milk, butter (2 TBSP.), sugar, and salt in a heavy saucepan and heat just to a simmer. Slowly add the cornmeal in a thin stream, whisking constantly. Lower the heat and continue stirring with a wooden spoon until the mixture has thickened and leaves the sides of the pan, about 10 minutes.

Pour into two 9x12" oblong baking dishes, cover with waxed paper, and refrigerate for one hour. Divide into pieces and fry in melted butter (4 TBSP.) at high heat to sear Polenta. Serve warm.

Mushrooms with Parmesan

****

Ingredients:

2 pound mushrooms, sliced

4 TBSP. butter or margarine

4 TBSP. flour

2 C. sour cream

1/2 tsp. salt, or to taste

Freshly ground pepper to taste

1 1/2 C. freshly grated Parmesan cheese

1/2 C. chopped parsley

DIRECTIONS:

Saute mushrooms in butter about 2 minutes. Add flour to sour cream; add cream mixture to mushrooms and heat until it begins to boil. Turn into a greased shallow baking dish. (Can be made ahead that day and refrigerated until baked at host's house.) Sprinkle with salt, pepper, Parmesan cheese, and parsley. Bake in preheated 425 degree oven 10 minutes, or until bubbly.

Refreshing Strawberry Wine Punch
****

Ingredients:

1 C. sugar

1 C. water

1 TBSP. finely shredded orange peel

1/2 C. orange juice

2 tsp. finely shredded lemon peel

1/4 tsp. lemon juice

4 cups sliced strawberries

1 bottle dry white wine

DIRECTIONS:

In a small saucepan combine the sugar and water; heat almost to a boiling point, stirring to dissolve sugar. Remove from heat; stir in citrus peels and juices. Chill. In a blender or food processor puree berries. Add to juice mixture; chill 30 minutes. Transfer to punch bowl; add wine. If desired, float a colorful berry-ladden ice ring on the top of the punch.

Brandied Apple Pecan Tart
****

Ingredients:
Crust:
1 1/2 C. flour
1/2 C. granulated sugar
1/4 tsp. salt
1/2 C. butter or margarine
1/3 C. pecans - finely chopped
Filling:
1/3 C. light brown sugar
1 TBSP. corn starch
1/4 tsp. cinnamon
2 TBSP. brandy
1 1/2 lbs. tart baking apples (Granny Smith - 4-6 apples), peeled and sliced 1/8" thick
Topping:

2 TBSP. light brown sugar
2 TBSP. chopped pecans

DIRECTIONS:

To make crust:
 Combine flour, sugar and salt in a large mixing bowl. Cut butter with knife or pastry blender until it resembles fine crumbs. Add pecans and mix. Press mixture into bottom and up one inch on sides of 9" springform pan. Set aside.

To make filling:
 In a large bowl combine brown sugar, corn starch and cinnamon. Mix. Stir in brandy. Add apples and toss to coat.

To assemble:
Arrange apples on top of crust in springform pan. Sprinkle top with brown sugar and pecans.e at 375 degrees for 40-50 minutes. Cool and top with sweetened whip cream or ice cream.